DETECTIVE ZACK

And The SECRET of Noah's Flood

JERRY D. THOMAS

Pacific Press® Publishing Association
Nampa, Idaho
Oshawa, Ontario, Canada

Edited by David C. Jarnes
Designed by Dennis Ferree
Cover and inside art by Kim Justinen
Typeset in 13/16 New Century Schoolbook

Library of Congress Cataloging-in-Publication Data:

Thomas, Jerry D., 1959-
    Detective Zack and the secret of Noah's flood / Jerry D. Thomas.
        p.   cm.
    Summary: Uses one ten-year-old boy's trip across the United
States, and the scientific clues he finds along the way, to suggest
that much of the evidence some interpret as pointing to an ancient
earth could also be viewed as evidence of the biblical Flood.
    ISBN 0-8163-1107-2
    1. Deluge—Juvenile literature. [1. Deluge.]   I. Title.
BS658.T48   1992
222'. 1106—dc20   92-5730
                                                          CIP
                                                           AC

04 05 06 07 08 • 14 13 12 11

Dedication

To my wife,
Kitty,
who is my inspiration,
and to my children:
Jonathan, Jennifer, and Jeremy.

Acknowledgment

The Geoscience Research Institute's field school
and materials provided many of the facts for
this book. And a special word of appreciation is
due to Dr. Ariel Roth and his staff, who took
time to review the manuscript.

Contents

CHAPTER ONE

Noah and the Tooth Fairy

**Daniel Boone National Forest
Twin Knobs Campground, Kentucky
June 27**

Why am I lying in my sleeping bag in a tent, writing in a notebook? What am I doing in Daniel Boone's forest? It's a long story, so I'll start at the beginning.

I'm trying to be still so I won't wake up my sister or brother, but it's not easy to write straight on this bumpy ground. Especially with a pencil in one hand and a flashlight in the other.

Anyway, it all started when my dad came home to tell us that we were going on a trip this summer. At first, I didn't want to go. I mean, I would miss out on summer camp and everything! But when he told me where we were going, I changed my mind. Because it's going to help me solve a mystery.

Really, I guess it started when my friend Bobby told me I was crazy. He wasn't being mean. He was just telling me what he thought. Friends are like that. And we're really good friends.

We have a fort in the woods behind my house. No one else knows where it is. One day, when we were building a secret lookout tower, I said something about Noah's ark.

"I wonder how this big rock got here?" Bobby had asked. He was standing on a rock that's bigger than my dad's van. It's the back wall of our fort, and our lookout station is on top.

"I'm sure the Flood left it there," I said as I carried another branch up to the top.

"What flood?"

"You know, the Flood. With Noah and the ark and everything?" I was sure he was teasing me.

"You're kidding me!"

I set the branch down and looked at him. "No, I'm not. How else do you think this rock got here?"

He laughed at me. "Nobody believes Noah and the Flood is a true story!"

"I do!"

"I guess you believe the Easter bunny and the tooth fairy are real too."

"What are you talking about? Don't you believe the stories in the Bible are real?" I thought he was just kidding. But he was being serious.

"Don't you know that scientists have proof that the world is millions of years old?"

"No, I never . . ."

"And they can prove that there never was a flood that covered the whole world."

I was getting confused. I knew that some scientists said those things, but I didn't think anyone believed them. "I don't think that's true. Who told you that?"

"We learned it in school. It's in my science book, so it has to be true."

"But the Bible says that Noah's flood really happened. How could the Bible be wrong?"

"My teacher says that the Bible is just an old storybook like Grimm's fairy tales or Mother Goose stories. She says that only some old-fashioned Christians still believe that stories like the Flood really happened. Are you an old-fashioned Christian?"

I didn't like being called old-fashioned. It sounded like old Mrs. Harper's dresses or a fire engine pulled by horses. But I didn't know what to say. I wanted to tell him to shut up, but that didn't seem right. Lucky for me, someone else spoke up.

"Zack, time for supper! Come home!" It was my mom.

"I gotta go," I mumbled and ran to my house.

I have to tell you, I was very confused. I thought everyone believed that the Bible was true, that the Flood was real. Right after Dad said the blessing, while he reached for the mashed potatoes, I threw the question at him.

"Dad, are the stories in the Bible true?"

Dad dropped the serving spoon into the gravy. My mom stopped pouring Kayla's juice and stared at me. Kayla's spoonful of corn stopped halfway to her mouth. (She's my sister and OK for a girl. But don't tell her I said so!) Even Alex stopped chewing for a minute (he's seven).

"What do you mean, Zack?" Dad fished out the spoon and used it to paint Kayla's potatoes with the brown gravy.

"I mean, are they real or just pretend—like fairy tales or Teenage Mutant Ninja Turtles?"

"Zack, we've always taught you that the Bible stories and people are real." Mom poured the juice as she talked. "Who told you they weren't?"

"Bobby told me that scientists can prove that the earth is millions of years old and that there never was a flood that covered the whole earth."

"And why do you think he might be right?" Dad asked.

"He said it was in his science book. And his teacher told him that the Bible was just an old storybook."

Dad looked across the salad bowl at me. Kayla was watching him too, waiting for his answer. Even Alex was listening.

"Part of what Bobby said is true."

"It is?" Kayla was shocked.

"Please let me finish." Dad looked sharply at her. "Bobby is right. Many scientists believe that the Bible is wrong, that there was no Flood. And most public schools don't teach that God created the earth and all the things that live on it. Instead, they teach evolution—the idea that over millions of years, the earth and the living things on it just kind of developed on their own."

"But can they prove it?" I asked.

"They think they can. But I think they're wrong."

"Can you prove that the Bible is right?"

"No. I can't prove it. That's why the Bible says we need faith. Zack, do you know what the Bible says faith is?"

"No."

This time Mom spoke up. "Zack, do you know what the word *evidence* means?"

"Isn't it like clues?"

"Yes. A detective looks for evidence or clues to solve a mystery. The Bible says that faith is the evidence of things not seen. What do you think that means?"

I chewed up a mouthful of mashed potatoes while I thought about that. "I guess it means that faith is believing something when there aren't enough clues to prove it."

"That's right, Zack."

"But if the whole world was covered with water, wouldn't there be some clues left behind? I wish I could tell Bobby some things that his scientists left out. Something that would show him that the Flood could have happened."

It was the next day when Dad came home with the good news about this summer.

But my flashlight batteries are running out! And I haven't even explained why I'm here or what I'm writing in my notebook. Well, I'll get to that tomorrow.

I'd better write myself a note to ask Dad for new batteries.

Interesting Things I've Seen

_____
_____
_____
_____
_____
_____

Important Words

Scientists: People who study all about science to find out how or when or why things happen (almost like detectives).

Faith: Believing in something even when there aren't enough clues to prove it.

Evidence: Clues about what really happened.

Detective: Someone who solves mysteries by searching for clues about what happened.

Evolution: The idea that the earth and the living things on it just kind of developed on their own over millions of years of time.

Noah's Flood Clues

_____
_____
_____
_____

Dad, I need batteries!

CHAPTER TWO

A Detective Takes the Case

**On the freeway
Driving through Kentucky
June 28**

You won't believe what I saw this morning! We were swimming in the lake at the campground, and I saw a big fish swimming right at the surface of the water! I called Kayla, and she saw it too. When it didn't disappear, we got closer. It swam away, but stayed at the top. We followed it around, and then some other kids joined us, and we tried to surround it and catch it. I grabbed it once, but it slipped away.

Near our campsite, I saw three deer eating grass. Their white tails went up like flags when they ran. We also saw one chipmunk, one woodchuck, and a lot of rabbits. Kayla and I picked some blackberries for lunch and skipped rocks on the lake.

Dad watched the rock-skipping for a minute; then he said, "See if you can hit that big green stump."

The stump was about as big as I am, but a lot more slimy! It was a long way out in the lake. Kayla couldn't throw that far, but I hit it—and when I did, it moved!

"Hey, Dad, look! The stump moved when I hit it."

He started throwing rocks too. And of course, he throws a lot harder than I do, so when he hit it, the stump really rocked.

"You're right, Zack. It's floating."

"Do stumps always float straight up like that, Dad?"

"I guess so. The roots are probably the heaviest part, so they stay down."

Anyway, after lunch, we packed up and drove off to find another campground. So now I'm riding in the van, and I'll try to write in my notebook again if the road isn't too bumpy.

But I still haven't explained why I'm writing in it. I didn't get to finish my story last night. Oh, yeah . . .

"Dad?"

"Yes, Zack."

"I need some more batteries for my flashlight."

"Your flashlight is already dead?"

"Well, first Alex used it on our way back from catching fireflies last night. And don't forget, I had it on when I was helping you find more wood for the fire."

"That's true, you were helping."

"Plus, I used it when Mom was looking for her sewing needle."

He looked over at Mom. "That's true," she said, "but we never did find it."

"And last night I had to use it to write in my notebook," I added.

"All right, all right," he laughed. "I think there are some new batteries in the camera case."

"Where's the camera case?"

"Well, I think it's right behind the seat, under the sleeping bags, right beside the cookstove. You can look for it when we stop at the next gas station."

DETECTIVE ZACK

By the time we pulled up to the pumps at a dusty gas station, I was ready . . . ready to jump out of the van and race to the restroom. And for once, I won and got there first. After that, of course, I had to see what kind of snacks and soda were for sale in the vending machines. Then Kayla ran up, tagged me, and shouted, "You're 'It'!"

Alex, Kayla, and I have been playing tag every time we stop. Kayla was "It" when we left after lunch, so she started this game. When Mom called us to the van, Alex was "It," so I'll have to watch out for him next time.

We were in the van and buckling our seat belts when I remembered the batteries. "Dad, wait a minute. I need to find those batteries."

Let me tell you something about our van. We were packed in like pickles in a pickle jar. It's not one of those big vans. It's just a minivan. With only one seat in the back, we had all the space behind it packed with food, clothes, and camping stuff. Usually, we argue about whose turn it is to sit by the door or by the window.

I looked at Alex and Kayla. They were already in their places and buckled up. Mom saw the argument coming. "Alex, Kayla, would you stand up for a minute so Zack can look for the camera case? Thanks, guys."

"Dad," I called out after a minute, "our tent's under the sleeping bags. I can't reach past it."

"Then you'll have to dig in from under the seat."

I looked at Mom. "Alex, Kayla," she said sweetly, "would you step out so Zack can look under the seat?"

They grumbled their way past me as I slid down to the floor in front. I pulled out a box of coloring books, a tape player, and my Micro Machines case. I thought I could see the camera case way in the back, so I stretched as far as I could and . . .

"Ouch! Mom!"

"What happened?"

"I think I found your needle."

I held up my right hand, with her needle sticking out of my finger. A little drop of blood was showing.

"Ow! I'm sorry." Her eyes were open wide, and she looked pale. Sometimes moms are like that.

"It's OK. It doesn't hurt that bad." I pulled out the needle and handed it to her. She held it away, like it was going to attack her next.

Anyway, I got the camera case and the batteries. Now, back to my notebook. I didn't get to finish last night, so I'll try to explain now. If I can keep from dripping blood on the pages.

DETECTIVE ZACK

Like I said, we had been talking about the Bible stories, especially Noah's flood. Did it really happen or not? I understood that there was no solid proof. It's not like someone was there to videotape it! But still, I wanted to know if there was some real evidence, some clues that it really happened.

That's when Dad came home with good news. He told us in the middle of pizza at supper one night. No, he wasn't in the middle of the pizza; we were just eating it when he told us. You know what I mean!

"How would you like to take a trip this summer?"

I thought of the trip we had taken the summer before. It was a nonstop drive to the school where Dad took summer classes. "Really, Dad, I'd like to stay home and go to summer camp with my friends and stuff like that."

"But we'll be going all the way to Utah."

"Where's Utah?" Alex wanted to know.

Dad got out the map of the United States. He traced a line with his finger all the way from our house in Maryland to Utah. "And look," he pointed out on the map, "we could stop in Texas and see your grandparents and cousins."

I liked that idea. But still, "Dad, why do you want to drive all the way to Utah?"

A Detective Takes the Case

"I can go to a different kind of class there this summer. The teachers are scientists who will be showing us evidence that the Bible is correct when it talks about Noah's flood."

That sounded even better. "You mean these scientists will show us clues that the Bible story about the Flood really happened?"

"Yes."

"What are we waiting for? Let's go!"

"Whoa!" Dad laughed. "It'll take time to get ready. We're going to camp all along the way in national parks and forests. So we'll need our tents and sleeping bags, and our cookstove and lantern. But, Zack," he added, "there's something I must do first. Come up here to the head of the table."

I wasn't sure I wanted to leave my pizza. Alex was close enough to grab it. But I kept an eye on it while I walked around to Dad's chair. He opened a paper bag and pulled out a brown explorer's hat and a blue pin with big letters that said "DETECTIVE ZACK."

"Zack," he said, "I name you detective on this case. It's your job to solve the mystery of Noah's flood. Could it have happened? Is there any evidence?"

He put the hat on my head. Everyone clapped and cheered. "Yaaaay!"

DETECTIVE ZACK

Then he reached into the bag again and pulled out a blue notebook, the same color blue as the pin. "Zack, like all good detectives, you must keep a list of all the clues. Write down everything you see and hear that might be important. Keep this notebook with you everywhere we go."

I took the notebook. "Thank you, Dad," I said. "I accept the case." I took off my hat and bowed like a person in a play.

"Yaaaay!" Everyone cheered again.

"Now, Zack," Dad said as I got back to my pizza, "if you write down every clue we find, when we get back, you'll have something to teach Bobby about science. And about the Bible!"

"All right!"

So now you know why I've been writing in my notebook. I'm keeping a list of all the interesting things I see every day. And the important words I hear. You never know what will turn out to be a clue that supports the story of Noah's flood. And a good detective never misses a clue!

Interesting Things I've Seen

A chipmunk
Three deer
A very strange fish
A woodchuck
A floating stump

Important Words

Noah's Flood Clues

CHAPTER THREE

A Cave and a Candle

Mammoth Cave National Park
Jellystone Park Campground, Kentucky
June 29

I'd been to caves before, but never one like Mammoth Cave. It was great! After standing around in the hot sun waiting for our tour to start, stepping into the cave felt good—like going into an air-conditioned store. I took off my detective hat to cool my head. The tour guide began explaining cave stuff right away.

DETECTIVE ZACK

"The strange rock formations [for-may-shuns] you will see are called stalactites [stah-lak-tights] and stalagmites [stah-lag-mights]. The ones hanging from the ceiling like icicles are stalactites. The ones growing up from the floor are stalagmites. Mammoth Cave is a living cave. That means that the stalactites and stalagmites are still growing. They are still being formed today, just like they have been for millions of years."

I looked at Dad. "Millions of years? We won't learn anything about Noah's flood here."

Dad turned toward me and winked. "Let's just listen and watch while we're here. Maybe we can find some hidden clues."

The tour guide was pointing to a stalactite that was almost touching a stalagmite. "Watch for the drip of water." We watched, and one drop fell. "As the drop of water passes over the formations, it leaves behind a tiny bit of the minerals it carries. Slowly those minerals build up on the surfaces. So, with every drop, the stalagmite grows a little taller and the stalactite grows a little longer. At the rate this water is dripping, we believe that these two will grow together in about ten thousand years."

Alex spoke loud enough for everyone to hear. "Is that a long time, Mom?"

A Cave and a Candle

The people on the tour all laughed. I was embarrassed. Little brothers are like that sometimes. "Let's not wait around to see," the tour guide said as she led the way farther down into the cave.

Soon we were in a big room. And when I say big, I mean big! It was big enough to put a whole football stadium in, including the seats and the lights!

The tour guide pointed to the tiny stream of water running along the bottom of the room. "It's hard to believe that a room this big could have been carved out of solid rock by a little stream like that, but it was. Over millions of years, that stream washed away this much rock!" She waved her arm around the room.

I'll say it's hard to believe, I thought.

"Now I want to give you an idea how this cave must have looked to the first explorers who came in." She moved over to a metal box. "In a minute, I'm going to turn out all the lights. It will be totally dark."

"Oooooh," everyone said.

"Then I'll light one candle to show you how much light the early cave explorers had. Children, don't leave your parents alone in the dark. They might get scared, and I don't want any crying parents to take care of."

DETECTIVE ZACK

Kayla grabbed my arm and stood close to me. I guess she was scared or something. Sisters are like that sometimes. I looked around and saw that Dad was standing next to Mom, holding Alex. We scooted over next to them. Just so they wouldn't worry.

"Everyone ready? Here we go!" The lights went out, and it was dark. I mean really dark. I couldn't tell if my eyes were open or closed! I couldn't see anything at all. I waved my hands in front of my face to see if I could see them.

"Ouch!"

"Sorry, Kayla."

Then the tour guide lighted the candle. The yellow light made giant shadows on the walls and ceiling.

"Oooooh," everyone said again.

The candlelight seemed a lot brighter than I thought it would.

"Now watch this." She used the candle to light a short torch. "Early explorers used torches to explore the dark passages. When they wanted to see how big a room like this was, they would do this." She swung her arm and threw the torch up to a ledge high above the floor.

"Oooooh," we all said.

The torch flickered brightly, and I tried to imagine exploring a cave like this. I bet Bobby and I could have done it.

"Mom, are there any caves near our house?"

"I hope not!" she exclaimed.

I wonder why she said that?

Later, back at the campground, we had a lot of fun too. There was a pool and a waterslide. We swam until it was nearly dark; then we changed and came back to the camp outdoor theater and watched Yogi Bear cartoons for a while. Then somebody put on a Yogi Bear costume and went around shaking hands with the little kids. The Yogi in the costume didn't look "smarter than your average bear," but I guess Alex liked him. Little brothers are like that.

It was dark by the time we started making supper. Dad lighted the lantern and set it on the picnic table so we could see. It was my turn to help Mom make supper. Dad, Kayla, and Alex started setting up the beds in the tents.

"Zack, the cookstove needs to be pumped up before we light it."

"No problem, Mom." I popped out the little handle and started pumping. It was harder than I thought. ". . . forty-eight, forty-nine, fifty. It's ready, Mom," I panted.

"Thanks. Now if you'll open the beans, I'll chop

the lettuce and tomatoes. And open a can of olives too."

I started twisting the stubborn can opener around the tops of the cans. "Mom," I asked, "what kind of candle do you think that was in the cave today? You remember, the one that guide lighted after the lights were out? I think it was brighter than this lantern!"

"It was a normal candle, Zack. It just seemed brighter because your eyes had adjusted to the darkness."

"What?"

"You know that the pupils in your eyes, the black part, get larger when it's dark."

"Yes."

"Well, the cave was so dark that your pupils got as large as they could. So when the candle was lighted, it seemed much brighter than usual."

"So if that candle were out here now, it wouldn't seem bright at all."

"No, not next to this lantern or the campfire. And maybe there's a good lesson in this, Zack. A lesson about truth."

I looked at Mom and shook my head. "I don't understand."

"People who don't know much about God and the beginning of this world might think that the scientists' stories of millions of years and no Flood are pretty bright ideas. But when you compare those ideas to the truth from the Bible, they seem pale and weak."

I looked at her eyes shining in the firelight. "Thanks, Mom, I like that. I want the real truth, not somebody's weak ideas. I'm glad we're going on this trip. I didn't get to ask Dad if he saw any hidden clues in the cave yet."

"I'm sure you'll have time tomorrow," she said. "We have to leave early and drive all day."

While I was giving her a hug, I saw something. "Hey, look! A bat!"

"What! Where?"

"It just swooped over the fire. Look, there it is again!"

Mom dived toward the tent, nearly knocking me down. "Keep it away from me!" she screamed.

"Aw, Mom. It's already gone. Come on, let's eat." I don't know what she was so upset about. It looked cute to me. I guess moms are just like that.

Interesting Things I've Seen

A big cave room

A totally *dark*, big cave room

A bright candle

A flying torch

A flying bat

Stalactites

Stalagmites

Important Words

Formations: Rocks in layers or shapes—sometimes weird shapes.

Stalactites: Rock formations hanging from the ceiling of a cave. They look like dirty icicles.

Stalagmites: Rock formations growing up from the floor of a cave. Many look like dirty, upside-down ice-cream cones.

Living cave: A cave in which the stalactites and stalagmites are still growing.

Minerals: The stuff in water that forms stalactites and stalagmites.

Noah's Flood Clues

CHAPTER FOUR

Tomato Plants and Muddy Feet

**Ouachita National Forest
Flatside Wilderness Campground, Arkansas
July 1**

I didn't get to write anything in the notebook last night. We had trouble finding the camping place, and by the time we stopped for the night, it was completely dark. That made it extra hard to set up the tents and make supper.

We just kept following a dirt road into the Ozark Mountains, and we ended up in the middle of nowhere. I mean, there was nothing and nobody for miles. We finally stopped at a large clearing on the side of a mountain. You'd have thought the place would be quieter than a schoolroom in summer. But when I got out of the car, so much noise blasted my eardrums that I couldn't hear myself think. It sounded like a chainsaw party at an airport!

"Where's all this noise coming from?" I shouted at Dad.

"It must be crickets and other insects! It was quieter in the car, with the engine running!"

We rushed around to set up the tents, and when we were finished, Kayla and I had a plan.

"Dad, let's take a flashlight and go see what's making all the noise," we shouted.

"OK. Let me set up the cookstove for your mother." He was ready in a few minutes, and we stalked off toward the nearest trees. When we got to the first tree, we shined the light at it. But the creature or creatures in it that were making the noise stopped—though you could barely tell because of the noise from the other trees.

"What is it? Do you see anything?" We searched through the tree but saw nothing except leaves. At the next tree, the same thing happened. We looked all through the branches and even on the ground under the tree, but we couldn't find anything.

"This time, let's sneak up on it," I shouted. So we turned off the flashlight and walked in the dark to the next tree. Then I snapped on the light, and we saw one of the noisemakers! It was a green tree frog, sitting on the edge of a green leaf, peeping at the top of its lungs. It wasn't any bigger than a quarter. There must have been thousands of frogs in those trees, all singing like crazy.

We shouted the story to Mom, and she was amazed too. Anyway, since we couldn't talk or anything, we went straight to bed after eating. When the sun woke me up in the morning, it was quiet. I looked for the tree frogs, but I couldn't find even one.

Yesterday, right after we crossed the Mississippi River, I remembered to ask Dad about the cave. I put on my detective cap and started asking questions.

"OK, Dad. How do we explain the millions of years it took to carve out a cave that big?"

"That's a good question, Zack. Let's start by thinking about how caves are formed. Usually, caves are found where the rocks underground are a kind of rock called limestone. Limestone dissolves slowly in water."

"What do you mean?" I asked. "Does it get soft and fall apart like mud?"

"Not exactly. It's more like a lollipop. It just gets smaller and smaller until it's gone. Anyway, as water seeps through the limestone . . ."

"What do you mean, seeps?"

"The water flows through and around the limestone. It's like my tomato plant on the back porch. You turn on the water hose and let some water trickle into the big pot, and pretty soon, the water is flowing out onto the ground from the holes in the bottom."

I remembered. "So that water seeps through from the top to the bottom."

"Right," Dad said. "Caves are being formed today the same way. When it rains, water seeps through the limestone and forms underground streams or rivers like you saw yesterday. And as the water slowly dissolves the limestone rock, the space inside—the cave—gets bigger."

"So that cave we were in is still growing," I said.

"Yes. So scientists have looked at how much it grows in one year and have decided that to get as big as it is, it must have been growing for millions of years," Dad explained.

"So, are they right?"

"Let me answer that like this. Do you remember

the tomato plants I raised on the back porch last summer?"

Uh-oh! I was afraid I knew where this story was going. "Yes."

"And do you remember the day I asked you to water them for me?"

I was right. That was not a good day. "Yes," I answered. "I turned the water on more than just a trickle and left it on too long."

"And?"

"And it blasted one tomato plant right out of the pot!"

Dad laughed. "Well, not really. But the water seeped through the dirt in the pot so fast and for so long that it washed all the dirt right out from around the plant's roots. And when enough dirt was washed out the bottom, the plant fell over."

I groaned. "I remember the mud that ran all over the porch floor."

"Now think about the cave again. If the same amount of water was seeping through every year, it would grow at the same speed every year. But what if a lot of water had to seep through? What if . . ."

"What if there was a flood!" I said quickly. "It would wash out the limestone much faster than it is washing out today."

"Right. If the flood covered the whole earth, then when it went down after the rain stopped, that water had to go somewhere. It would be flowing down through big rivers and seeping quickly into rocks like limestone and carving out big caves in a short time."

"So caves are a pretty good clue that there was a flood," I agreed. "It makes a lot more sense that a flood of water washed out those rocks instead of just a drip. That makes the millions of years seem like a pretty pale idea!" I looked at my mom, and she smiled. "But wait a minute. What about the stalactites and stalagmites? The tour guide said they took millions of years to grow."

Dad had to think about it for a minute. "OK. What do we do when the dog wants to come into the house, and his feet are muddy?"

Murphy, our dog, has hairy feet, and he always finds mud even when it's not raining. "We put him in the bathtub and wash his feet off."

"And the bathtub is coated with mud."

"I know. I have to rinse it out," I groaned.

"What would happen if we never rinsed it out? What if the water always ran out, but not the mud?"

"The mud would get thicker and thicker on the bottom of the tub."

"Right. Now, if you washed the dog's feet every day, how long would it be until the tub was full of mud?"

That didn't make sense at first. "How would I know?"

"Think about it."

"Well, it depends on how dirty his feet are."

"That's right. The dirtier his feet are, the faster the tub would fill with mud. Now, stalactites are formed as the minerals in the water stick while the water drips off. So what do Murphy's dirty feet have to do with stalactites?"

"The dirtier the water is—I mean, the more minerals and stuff in it—the quicker the stalactites would grow," I figured out.

"And what do you think the floodwater would look like? All clean and pure?"

"No! It would be muddy and full of minerals and junk. Just right for growing stalactites. So stalactites and stalagmites are good clues that there was a flood too."

"Right you are, son. And of course, those stalactites and stalagmites have been growing since the Flood too."

"Thanks, Dad, for helping me understand. And . . . Dad?"

"Yes?"

DETECTIVE ZACK

"Sorry about your tomato plant last year."
"That's OK. I already forgot about it."
I guess dads are just like that.

Interesting Things I've Seen

Thousands of green tree frogs (But I only saw one.)

Important Words

Limestone: A kind of rock that can be dissolved by water.

Noah's Flood Clues

Caves: Large caves could have been washed out of the soft limestone faster if a lot of water was seeping through, like it would be if there was a flood.

Stalactites and stalagmites: Dirty floodwater, full of minerals, could have helped them grow faster than they are growing today.

CHAPTER FIVE

Wind, Rocks, and Dinosaur Walks

**Clayton Lake State Park
Clayton, New Mexico
July 10**

I haven't written in my notebook for a long time. I haven't really looked for any clues since our stop in Texas to see my grandparents and all my cousins. But I did see some very interesting things that I need to write down. And I will, if I can keep the wind from blowing my notebook away!

45

DETECTIVE ZACK

This campsite is neat. We set our tents up right next to the lake. But the really interesting things are the rocks. All around us stand big rocks that have weird, round shapes. One is as tall as a basketball goal, but it's shaped like a loaf of bread. Some are as big as cars or houses.

Walking between these big rocks is like walking down the streets of a big city and looking up at round skyscrapers and buildings. Except the rocks aren't *that* tall. And they're a lot of fun to climb!

Kayla, Alex, and I climbed to the top of one big rock that was shaped like a giant mushroom. We waved at Mom and Dad back at the campsite. "Hey, Dad!" I yelled. "What shaped all these rocks like this?"

"I can't hear you!" he yelled back. So when we finished climbing and went to eat, I asked him again.

Instead of answering, he asked me a question. "What do you think the tour guide at the cave would say?"

"I don't know, but probably that it took millions of years."

He laughed. "You're right. Scientists might tell you that at one time, this area was all level ground."

Alex was listening. He asked, "Did the rocks all grow here?"

"No," Dad said. "When the ground here was level, it was level with the tops of those rocks. Where we are sitting would have been twenty feet under the ground."

I looked out over the lake. "So the lake wasn't here then either."

"Not like it is now, anyway. Some of the rocks here were hard and some soft. Many scientists will tell you that over millions of years, the softer rocks were worn away by the rain and the wind. Now only the harder rocks are left. When the wind and rain wear away rocks and soil, it's called erosion [e-row-shun]."

"So that's why the rocks are in such weird shapes," I said. "When the soft parts washed away, the hard parts were just left hanging around. But I'd say the Flood washed the soft rocks away, not millions of years."

"I think you're right," Dad agreed. "The Bible says that when the rain stopped, God sent a great wind to dry up the earth. I think that wind and the floodwaters washed out the soft rocks and left this like we see it today."

So here I am, with a strong wind trying to blow the pages right out of my notebook. Now, back to the things I saw in Texas.

On that first night, we went to my grandma's house. She took us to an amusement park, Six Flags Over Texas, with all our aunts and uncles and cousins. The rides were neat! But I stayed off the roller coasters. I knew they would make me throw up!

Then, that weekend, we went to a place where you can see dinosaur tracks in the rocks. The tracks run right down the middle of a dry creek bed. We hiked out there and tried to follow in the footsteps.

"Hey, Mom, look at me!" Alex called out. He was standing with both feet in one dinosaur footprint! I could put both of my feet in one too. We tried to step from one footprint to the next, but they were too far apart.

"And this was not even a very big dinosaur," Dad laughed.

"Were there really big dinosaurs, Dad?" Alex asked.

"I think so, Alex. Scientists have found very big bones that belonged to some large beasts."

"I know," I added. "I've seen their skeletons in a museum."

"I have too," Dad said. "But usually when dino-saur bones or fossils are found, there are only a few pieces lying around together. The scientists have found only a few whole skeletons, so sometimes they guess what the whole skeleton would look like. And then they guess what the dinosaur would look like if it were alive."

"So there was no such thing as a tyrannosaur or a stegosaurus?"

"Probably there was. But with some of the other kinds, we don't know for sure. Sometimes it's almost as hard as looking at a pile of Legos and guessing what kind of truck you could make."

I thought of another question. "Dad, don't scientists say that dinosaurs lived millions of years before there were any people?"

"Yes. That's what some of them say."

Alex spoke up. "Daddy, what does the Bible say about dinosaurs?"

"The Bible doesn't say anything about dinosaurs, Alex."

"So doesn't that mean that there never really were any dinosaurs?"

"No. Dinosaurs could have lived on the earth before the Flood. They could have lived after the Flood, but not in the place where the people in the Bible lived. Or maybe they died during the Flood."

"I guess there wasn't any room for them on the ark!" Alex said.

Dad laughed. "Not all dinosaurs were giant creatures. Many dinosaurs were no bigger than your dog, Murphy."

I guessed, "Maybe they just didn't come when Noah called!"

The other fun stuff we did was fireworks on the Fourth of July at the house of my other grandparents. At Papa and Mema's (that's what we call them), we set off firecrackers and skyrockets. Lots of our cousins were there too.

We took a trip to the beach the next week. I was exploring the beach while Dad and Papa went fishing on a pier. I searched through tons of seashells and found a whole sand dollar. When I ran down the pier to show Dad, he and Papa were walking back toward me.

"Look what I found!" I shouted. While they were looking at it, I asked, "Did you catch anything?"

Dad was just saying, "No, we haven't even had a bite," when we heard someone far down the pier shouting.

"Hey, one of your fishing poles just went over the side!"

We ran as fast as we could to the place where they had left their poles. Sure enough, one of them was gone. And the other one was bending toward the water. Dad grabbed it quickly and started pulling back on the line.

"Whatever it is, it's big!" he said.

"It could be a shark," Papa said. "I've seen some big ones pulled in here."

"A shark!" I shouted. "Pull it in, Dad. I want to see it!"

"I'm trying," he grunted as he strained on the pole. Slowly it lifted, until suddenly, right on top of the water, we could see what he'd caught. But it wasn't a shark. It was a stingray!

"Wow!" I said. The ray was wider than I am tall. "Hold it there, Dad." But the stingray was tired of bothering with us. With a flip of his fins, he was gone. The fishing line snapped like a thread.

"I've never seen one like that," Papa said. "It was worth losing a fishing pole to see it."

But when Dad reeled in his broken line, Papa's pole came in too. The stingray had tangled them up together.

Pretty cool, don't you think?!

Interesting Things I've Seen

Rocks shaped like big loaves of bread and giant mushrooms

Millions of seashells

A sand dollar—a sea creature skeleton that looks like a silver dollar coin

A stingray

Important Words

Erosion: The wearing away of rocks and soil by wind and rain.

Noah's Flood Clues

Weird-shaped rocks: They could have been formed when the floodwaters went down and God sent wind to dry the land.

CHAPTER SIX

The Top of the World Is Wet

**Pike National Forest
Top of the World Campground, Colorado
July 11**

If I can keep from dripping on the pages, I'll try to write down what has happened since yesterday. I sure learned one thing, though—it's cold in the mountains, especially when you're wet.

Our first stop yesterday was at a place called the Garden of the Gods. It's a big park filled with gigantic slabs of rock. The ranger at the visitor center said that they were made of red and white sandstone. Anyway, these slabs, mostly great big, flat rocks standing on end, were in weird shapes.

We found that many of these strange shapes had names. "What do they call that one, Dad?" I asked. It looked like four shark fins sticking out of a big whale's back.

"I believe that it's called 'Kissing Camels.' "

"Kissing Camels?" I said. "That's a dumb name. Probably named by some girl." Kayla hit me.

We drove around the park, and Mom pointed out the other famous rocks. "And that one is called 'Cathedral Spires.' I guess someone thought it looked like church steeples."

"Look out, Dad!" Alex yelled.

Dad swerved from one side of the road to the other. "What is it? Look out for what?"

"Up there! That rock is going to fall on the road." Alex pointed to a big, round rock, way up on the edge of a cliff.

"Alex, that rock is called 'Balanced Rock.' It's been sitting there for years without falling. It just looks like it will fall any minute," Mom explained.

From the park, we could see Pike's Peak, the highest mountain in that area. It was a good thing we looked at it when we did. The peak was soon covered with clouds. In fact, dark clouds were slowly filling the sky. After lunch, we drove up into the mountains to find a camping spot.

When we pulled up to the campsite, we could hear thunder rumbling. "Zack, we'd better set up those tents in a hurry," Dad said.

He and I jumped out and quickly went to work. Just about the time we got everything out of the car, the rain started. "Where do we set the tents up now?" I shouted.

"As long as it's not in a hole, it doesn't really matter. Every place will be wet soon." Dad grabbed the hammer and the stakes. "Put the sleeping bags and other stuff back in the van until the tents are ready."

To make a wet story short, we ate supper standing up under the back hatch of the van and then crawled into our damp tents. The rain kept falling, and it sounded like we were on the inside of a drum. "Daddy," Alex called out, "come in and tell us a story."

Mom and Dad both crawled into our tent. Alex sat in Mom's lap, and Dad crawled in between Kayla and me. Lightning flashed around us, and the mountain rumbled with thunder.

"Daddy, will the lightning strike us here?" Kayla was worried.

"I think we'll be safe, honey. Don't worry."

I tried to help. "Kayla, there's no way lightning could strike us here."

"Why?"

"We're up in the clouds, and the lightning is striking down at the ground." That sounded good until a flash of lightning as bright as day shook the mountain under us. The rain kept drumming on the tent roof. We all huddled closer together.

Dad spoke up. "Do you think Noah and his family felt like this that first night the ark floated in the Flood? They must have been scared too."

Mom added, "And the whole world outside the ark's door was being destroyed. Their home and everything were gone. All they had left was their faith in God's promise to save them."

"I know what they felt good about," Alex spoke up. "They had lots of animals to play with."

"Ha," I laughed, "and lots of animals to clean up after!"

"And what about breakfast?" asked Mom. "How would you like a hungry elephant trumpeting you awake?"

"Or a lion roaring? Or an eagle screaming?" Kayla added. Alex just smiled and nodded. Little brothers are like that.

"Zack," Dad said, "there is some evidence for Noah's flood that we can't see on a trip like this.

But it's important, so you might want to write it in the notebook."

Luckily, my notebook was in my pillowcase. I had left my hat in the car so it would stay dry. "OK, tell me."

"All right. The Bible isn't the only book that tells about a worldwide flood. There are flood stories from nearly every old civilization [civi-li-za-shun]."

"What's a civilization?" Kayla asked.

"It's a group of people who live together and form their own way of life. The children of Israel in the Bible were one of the old civilizations. In every part of the world, people had their own ways and their own stories. But most of them tell about a flood that covered the earth and destroyed everything."

"Are all the flood stories like the one in the Bible?" I asked.

"No. They are all different. There are different heroes and different reasons why the flood came. Remember, none of the other old civilizations worshiped the true God."

"Why is that good evidence for Noah's flood?" asked Kayla.

"Kayla, what if you ran into the visitor center at Garden of the Gods and told the rangers that you saw two real camels kissing outside?"

She laughed. "No one would believe me."

"But what if all of us said we saw them too?"

She thought. "Well, I'm sure some people would believe us. But some would think we were all crazy."

"OK, but what if ten or twenty other people came in and said they saw kissing camels too? Don't you think the rangers would believe it then?" She nodded, and he went on. "The same is true for the flood stories. When so many people tell of a flood that covered the earth, so many people who don't even know each other, it makes it seem likely that a big flood really happened."

I spoke up. "Did all the stories come from the people who lived near the Israelites? Could it have been just a really bad flood in that area?"

"Seven flood stories come from the Middle East area. But three come from Africa, and six come from South America. And the North American Indians told thirteen different stories of a flood."

"Wow! You almost have to believe that something big happened all over the world."

"That's right," Dad said. "Now listen. The rain has stopped, and maybe the storm is over. Everyone go to sleep, and we'll probably wake up to beautiful, blue skies."

Interesting Things I've Seen

"Kissing Camels"
A balanced rock (It looked like it was about to fall.)
More strange rock shapes

Important Words

Sandstone: Rock made up of sand cemented together.
Civilization: A group of people who live together and form their own way of life.

Noah's Flood Clues

Flood stories: Stories of a worldwide flood were told in old civilizations all over the world—so something probably happened to the whole world.

CHAPTER SEVEN

Mountains and Waterfalls

**Colorado National Monument
Saddlehorn Campground, Colorado
July 12**

It was a great summer day at camp. I was just floating away on my tube in the lake, dipping my hands and feet into the water, splashing a little on my face. But wow, this water was cold. Too cold. And why was I so cold, there in the sunshine? What in the world, I thought . . . and zap, just like that, I was awake. But I was still floating in water. Well, almost. My pillow was soaked, and my sleeping bag was wet down to my knees.

I rolled over and looked up just in time to catch a big cold drop right in the eye. The tent was leaking right at the top of the door zipper. "Oh, yuck," I said out loud.

"Zack, is that you? Come on out and help me build a fire." Dad was already carrying wet wood up to the campfire pit. I got my damp coat on and went out to help. The sky rumbled and flashed, and the fire wouldn't start no matter what we did.

Soon other voices were calling out from the tents. "Hey, it's wet in here." "Is the fire going yet?" "What's for breakfast?" And just as they stepped out into the morning cold, the rain started again.

Everyone dashed for the van. The doors slammed, the engine roared, and we sat shivering as we waited for the heat to come on. "You know, Zack, we might as well go out and pack up the tents now, since we're wet anyway," Dad said.

I guess he was right. It was a good plan. Until the hail started falling. Bonk, a hail stone bounced off my head. Mom opened her window and shouted, "Just wad it all up and throw it in. We'll drive to a laundromat and dry it all there."

So we did it as quickly as we could and were

soon inching our way back down the mountain toward the big city of Denver and the nearest clothes dryers.

After a quick change of clothes and breakfast at a McDonald's, we found a laundromat and filled every dryer. Dad and I were out in the parking lot, folding up the wet tents. He said, "We must look pretty strange to people driving by."

"I don't care," I said. "I'd rather look strange than feel wet and cold."

Later, after everything was dry and clean, we had lunch at Casa Bonita. That place is wild! We ate our food next to the waterfall. Yes, there really is a waterfall, right in the restaurant. And every few minutes, a diver would step out beside the falls and dive into the pool at the bottom. Also, there were arcade games, puppet shows for little kids, and "Black Bart's Cave," where you had to fight your way past pirates and giant spiders to find the treasure (not really, but it was fun to pretend).

Soon we were headed west again, toward Utah. I was staring at the mountains as we climbed higher and higher. But something seemed wrong. "Dad, why is everyone passing us?"

"The van has a problem. You remember how it was losing power yesterday? Well, it's worse now.

The higher we go in the mountains, the less power the engine has."

"Why? Is it just harder to pull all of our stuff?"

"No, it has to do with oxygen [ox-e-jen]. Car engines breathe in oxygen just like we do. The higher you go, the less air there is—so the less oxygen. You'll find that out when we get to Utah and you start to run and play. You'll get tired and out of breath quickly."

"Will we be staying on a mountain in Utah?"

"Yes, right at the top. Anyway, when the van doesn't get enough oxygen, it can't burn the gas very well, so it doesn't have much power."

All this time, we were going slower and slower. "Is our van going to make it over the mountains?" I asked.

"We'll know soon. This is the highest part right ahead of us. If we can get to the top, I'm sure we'll make it to Utah." Dad turned on the blinkers and stayed close to the right side of the road so others could go by.

I wasn't sure we would make it, but slowly we climbed to the top—and picked up speed going down the other side. Soon we were looking for the turnoff to our campsite.

"We're not really going up there, are we?" Mom was pointing up at the cliffs toward which we were headed. When we began climbing up the side of the cliff on a small, curvy road, I could tell by the look on her face that she wasn't very happy.

The campground was right up on the clifftop, called a plateau (plah-tow). It was a wide area, as flat as a table, with nothing but rocks and short bushes. After the tents were set up, I wanted to go exploring, but Mom insisted that we all stay together.

We walked together toward the edge of the cliff, where a ranger was pointing out something to some other campers. "These monoliths [monn-o-liths]—these tall, skinny fingers of stone—were formed by millions of years of the wind and rain's erosion." I looked out at one of the big rock statues. It looked about as big as a tennis court on top, and the sides went almost straight down. "That big one there," the ranger said, pointing to an enormous rock standing out by itself, "is called Independence [in-d-pen-dents] Rock. It is 500 feet tall."

"Oooooh," everyone said.

"Once this whole area was level with us here. But now, all that is left is this plateau and these majestic rocks. Isn't it amazing what millions of years of erosion can do?" The ranger laughed as he walked away.

DETECTIVE ZACK

"Either millions of years or lots of water!" Dad said, and he winked at me. We walked on and saw "Window Rock," a rock monolith with a hole right through it. There was also one called the "Devil's Kitchen." It was probably named by a mother who was tired of cooking on camping trips.

"Look at that!" Alex said, pointing to the edge of the cliff. "A squirrel just ran off the edge." But the squirrel popped back up as he said it. While we watched, several more rock squirrels ran along and over the edge and back up. "See, Mom," Alex said, "the squirrels aren't afraid." Mom just shuddered and grabbed his hand.

At the evening program, the ranger told more about the history of the area and its first explorers. Later, we walked back to our tents in the dark. Well, it wasn't really dark, because the full moon was shining out of a clear sky. No clouds were in sight, I was happy to notice.

"Stay close together," Mom said. "I don't want anyone falling over the edge."

Of course, we were probably a thousand feet from the edge, but it was nice to know that she cared. Moms are just like that, I guess.

Suddenly, something "whooshed" past us in the air. "What was that?" cried Kayla.

"A bat!" Mom yelled. "Run!"

Now I was afraid that *she* was going to jump over the edge. "Just be still," Dad said. "Listen. It's not a bat. Hear the wind in its wings? It's a nighthawk."

Then we saw it clearly in the moonlight. And it was a nighthawk, out eating mosquitoes and other bugs. In fact, we saw seven more before we got back to the tents.

"Well, it could have been a bat," Mom said, watching the sky carefully. After our worship and prayer, we got into our sleeping bags. She zipped them all the way up. "No sleepwalking tonight, you guys," she said.

"Aw, Mom, go to bed," I said. Poor Mom. With "bats" and "cliffs" all around her, I wonder if she slept at all.

Interesting Things I've Seen

Waterfall divers
"Black Bart's cave"
Seven rock squirrels
Eight nighthawks

Important Words

Oxygen: What we must breathe to stay alive. Cars need it too.
Plateau: Flat land on a mountain.
Monoliths: Very tall rocks.

Noah's Flood Clues

CHAPTER EIGHT

Clues From a Dinosaur's Lunch

**Brian Head Ski Resort
Brian Head, Utah
July 13**

"Utah at last!" Dad said as we crossed the state border this morning.

"How much farther to the place we're going?" I asked. We'd never really talked about where in Utah Dad's classes were being taught.

"It's still about six hours to Brian Head. It's way down in the southwest corner of the state."

"Brian who?" asked Alex.

"Not Brian who, Alex, Brian Head," I tried to explain. "It's just the name of the place, not a person."

"I wish we had time to go by Dinosaur National Monument. It's not too far from here," Dad said.

"Do they have real dinosaurs there?" Alex asked.

"No. It's really a dinosaur graveyard. More dinosaur bone fossils have been found there than any other place on earth."

"I never thought of dinosaurs living here in America," I said. "Did they find any whole skeletons or just pieces?"

"I believe that fifteen whole skeletons have been found, and parts of many others. And there are still more being dug up every year. If you could go there, you could watch the paleontologists [pay-lee-un-tall-uh-jists] working to remove the fossils from the ground. Paleontologists are scientists who study bones and fossils."

"Are you sure we don't have time to go there?" Kayla asked.

"Sorry, but my classes start tomorrow. We need to get to Brian Head this afternoon."

I was curious about that dinosaur graveyard. "Dad, how did all those dinosaur bones get to that one spot?"

Clues From a Dinosaur's Lunch

"That's a good question, Zack. First of all, scientists think that many of the dinosaurs of earth died suddenly. They aren't sure why. But they believe that there was a large river flowing through what is now the graveyard. For whatever reasons, when the dinosaurs in this area died, many of their bodies fell into the river and floated downstream to the point where the bones are found today. At that place, the river became clogged up, and the dinosaur bodies were eaten or sank."

"It would take a pretty big river to float dinosaurs, wouldn't it?"

Dad laughed. "Yes, it would. Anyway, the scientists think that after a long time, the sand and mud where the dinosaurs sank became rock. And the dinosaur bones became fossils when the sand or mud turned into rock, because the skeleton turned to stone also."

I thought about that. It was time for a little detective work. "Now wait a minute. The dinosaurs died suddenly; then their giant bodies floated away to be covered with sand and mud that turned into rock. Doesn't that sound like Noah's flood to you?"

"It does to me," Dad agreed. "The story of the flood fits the scientific facts of the case. Some paleontologists may have other ideas about what happened, but the Bible's flood story makes the most sense to me."

"It would take a flood just to float those big, fat dinosaur bodies away and pile them up," Alex added.

"And I'll give you another clue," Dad said. "If those dinosaurs lived near this area before they died, what do you think they ate?"

I could only guess. "Probably either each other or some kind of plants."

"The dinosaurs they found were ones that ate plants. But though they have found lots of dinosaur fossils, they have found very few plant fossils—and nothing much that could have fed dinosaurs' huge appetites. What does that tell you?"

"Well, it must mean that those dinosaurs didn't live near here. They must have lived somewhere else," I decided.

"There is little fossil evidence of dinosaur food anywhere in those rocks. So they must have lived a long way from where they were found," Dad said.

"That makes sense if you believe in a flood that covered the whole world." I got busy writing in my notebook.

Clues From a Dinosaur's Lunch

Later that afternoon, we found the mountain road that led to Brian Head. We stopped in the small town there and asked a mechanic what could be done for our van's mountain troubles.

"The cars of the people who live here have been adjusted for high mountains. You could have your van adjusted—but that would be expensive, and you'd have to have it adjusted back when you leave. So you probably don't want to do that. The only thing you can do if it just won't go is to pull over and turn the engine off for a few minutes. When it cools down, it'll run better again." The mechanic wished us luck, and we left for the mountains.

Looking up the road, Mom asked, "Do you think the van will make it? It's steeper than any other road we've been up."

Dad shrugged. "All we can do is try. And pray."

I know I prayed. I'm sure they did too. But it wasn't long until the van began to slow down. Dad steered to the right side and kept going. Finally, we were just inching along. He pulled over at the next safe place.

"Well, here we sit until it cools down. Anyone else want a sandwich?" He opened the ice chest and began building a meal.

I explored around the road for a few minutes,

but I was bored and ready to go when he started the van again. We drove on for a mile or two, but soon we slowed down again.

"Dad, I think that bug is passing us. It might be time to stop," I suggested.

"Let's try to make it over this next hump," he replied. We just barely made it. And there below us was the town of Brian Head. Best of all, it was in a nice, almost flat meadow. We sputtered around until we found the place where we were staying.

Dad had a big surprise for us. We weren't going to be staying in a hotel room. Instead, our "room" was a whole apartment, with three bedrooms, a kitchen, and two bathrooms. Brian Head is a ski resort, and in the summers, they rent out the skiers' apartments.

"Dad, I love camping, but this is going to be a nice break. Hot showers every day, soft beds, and even cable TV! And hot meals three times a day." I was one happy camper. "Not that I didn't like what you cooked, Mom."

"It's OK, dear. I think I can get used to this place too." She looked very happy.

Later, we explored the rest of the building while Dad went to check in with his teachers. "Hey, Mom, look! A hot tub! Can we go swimming?"

"I'm sure we can spend a few minutes relaxing

when your father gets finished. Let's go back and change while we wait."

For once I'm writing at a nice desk under a good light. No raindrops or mosquitoes will be bothering me tonight! Tomorrow, Dad starts his field trips to find more evidence of Noah's flood. Of course, I'll be along to catch all the clues. So I'd better get to sleep. If I *can* sleep on a soft bed anymore. Well, all I can do is try!

Interesting Things I've Seen

_____
_____
_____
_____
_____
_____
_____

Important Words

Paleontologists: Scientists who study bones and fossils to learn about animals or plants that lived long ago.

Fossils: Animals or plants—or parts of them—that have turned into rock.

Noah's Flood Clues

Dinosaur bones: Fossil dinosaur bones have been found all piled in one place by a lot of water. Very few plant fossils are found nearby, so the dinosaur bodies must have come from far away. This sounds like Noah's flood.

_____
_____
_____
_____
_____
_____

CHAPTER NINE

Whistling Woodchucks

Field trip
Cedar Breaks National Monument, Utah
July 16

It's been wonderful waking up in a dry, soft bed for a few days. And not having to pump the cookstove to make breakfast. I've even been able to catch up on my cartoon watching. But I'm glad that today is Dad's field trip to Cedar Breaks and that I get to go with him. I'm taking along my notebook in case I see something I need to write down.

DETECTIVE ZACK

"I think we should all go along on the trip," Mom had said at first. "It'll be fun."

"That's a great idea," Dad agreed. "It's only two miles from here, and the view is supposed to be beautiful from the cliffs. We're going to hike around the top of the—"

"Did you say cliffs?" Mom asked. "And you're going to walk along the edge? I think I'll stay here and rest, dear. You go ahead."

She grabbed Kayla and Alex to be sure that they weren't going. She almost grabbed me too, but I escaped with a promise to be careful. I left quickly in case she was thinking about changing her mind.

While I waited in the van, I found my cap and Dad's map, and by the time he got there, I was ready to roll. "Think the old van will make it?" I asked, patting the dashboard.

"Sure it will. Besides, it's only two miles away. We could always walk back." So we sputtered off behind the other cars. Soon we were parked at the first Cedar Breaks scenic overlook. We walked up to the edge with the other people from Dad's class and looked out over the cliff.

"Oooooh," everyone said.

One of the scientist-teachers started to explain. "The Cedar Breaks basin is more than 2,000 feet deep and three miles across." They call it a basin because it's bowl-shaped. It looks kind of like a football stadium with one end open. And we were standing on the top edge, where the highest seats would be. Except much, much higher.

It's hard to describe what Cedar Breaks looks like. From where we stood, we saw ridges of rock and deep canyons flowing toward the open end. The Cedar Breaks basin may look like a football stadium, but the rocky ridges look like lines of weird, lumpy, upside-down carrots. And these carrots have a lot of strange shapes. Some look like statues, some look like church steeples, and some are shaped like arches. (No, not like McDonald's. More like a horseshoe.) And they are all striped with dark red, light purple, and dull yellow.

"Wow," I said. "Mom's going to be sorry she missed this."

Dad agreed. "No wonder the Indians called this place 'the Circle of Painted Cliffs.' "

"Why do we call it Cedar Breaks? Are all the trees broken or something?"

"No," Dad laughed. "Early settlers got part of the name from the trees. Most of the trees here are a kind of cedar called juniper. But the second half of the name comes from the land. The settlers called this kind of land, with bare rocks and cliffs, *badlands* or *breaks*. That's how they got the name 'Cedar Breaks.'"

We followed the teacher down a path that ran along the top of the cliff but not too close to the edge. "What are we going to see, Dad?" I asked.

"We are going to see one of the oldest trees in the world."

"You mean a redwood tree?"

"No, that's the tallest kind of tree. The Great Basin bristlecone pine is the oldest," Dad said.

Just as we were stepping around a juniper log, I heard a sharp whistle. Who was that, I wondered. Then I heard it again. And I saw what was whistling. A short, fat animal was sitting right on the very edge of the cliff. Suddenly, it dropped out of sight!

"Dad, what kind of animal was that?" As I pointed, its head popped up over the cliff and it whistled again.

"That's a marmot. It's similar to a woodchuck. They whistle to warn each other of danger."

"Do they all live right on the edge of cliffs?"

"That's their favorite spot. I guess they feel safe there," he said.

We hiked out along one of the ridges toward a dead-looking tree. But up close, I could see some green branches. The teacher stopped and began to explain.

"This is the bristlecone pine. It looks almost dead, and the truth is, part of it is dead. But that's why the bristlecone pine lives so long. While one part dies, another part grows. So part of the tree is very old, and part is very young."

"How old is this tree?" someone asked.

"This one is more than 1,600 years old."

"Oooooh," everyone said.

"But other Great Basin bristlecone pine trees in the Southwest are probably more than 4,500 years old."

"Oooooh," everyone said again.

I walked up and touched the branches. It was hard to believe that this tree sprouted not long after Jesus' disciples lived. It was old when Columbus came to America! While I was walking around it, I saw another marmot near the cliff edge. I stepped slowly toward it to see how close I could get.

"Help! Oh, dear," I heard someone behind me say. I looked around to see what was the matter.

"I can't look. He's going to fall," the woman's voice said. I didn't see anyone in danger. Who is she talking about, I wondered.

"Zack, please come back up here," Dad said

quietly. "You're scaring that poor woman to death."

Me? She was worried about me? I wasn't even close to falling into the canyon. "Oh, brother," I said under my breath. "And I thought my mother was a worrywart."

Next we drove out into the countryside and stopped near a small mountain. The teacher led the group up to the top. I kind of dragged along behind, throwing rocks and kicking shells. All of a sudden, it hit me. Shells? I reached down and picked up a larger rock. It had seashells stuck in it.

"Hey, Dad," I called out. I had to run up the hill after him. "Look! What are seashells doing here?"

"That's what the teacher was just saying. This hill is covered with rocks and shells from the ocean. What do you think that means, Detective Zack?" he asked.

"That must mean that all this land was once covered with water," I answered.

"Yes. But it might not have been a mountain then."

"What do you mean?" I asked.

"Mountains like these are formed when the layers of rock far down inside the earth push up. It's hard to understand what those rocks down in the earth are doing. But they push up, and that forms mountains in long rows, like the Rocky Mountains we are in now."

"So this land could have been low and flat like the beach?"

"Yes, and scientists who believe in evolution might explain these shells by saying that this land was once at the bottom of the ocean."

"You mean this mountain used to be at the bottom of the ocean? And what's the bottom of the ocean now used to be the tops of some mountains?"

Dad nodded. "Scientists have found water-formed rocks and shells on mountains in countries all over the world. You can even find them on Mount Everest, the highest mountain in the world."

"Then," I said, "something must have turned this world inside out."

"If Noah's flood really happened, that's what you would expect to find," he replied. "That much water would have completely changed the earth. These mountains could have been pushed up during or after the Flood."

It's a good thing I brought my notebook. And a good pencil.

Interesting Things I've Seen

Two marmots

A very old tree (bristlecone pine)

Weird, lumpy rocks that look like upside-down carrots

Seashells on a mountain

Important Words

Basin: Bowl.

Breaks: A land of bare rocks and cliffs—also called badlands.

Marmot: A woodchuck that whistles and that lives in the mountains.

Bristlecone pine: The oldest trees in the world. Some are more than 4,500 years old.

Noah's Flood Clues

Seashells on mountains: Mountains all over the world have shells and water-formed rocks on them. And if some mountains were pushed up from the ocean floor, then something must have happened that completely changed the whole earth. I think it was Noah's flood.

CHAPTER TEN

Deep Canyon, Deep Trouble

**Picnic trip
Zion National Park, Utah
July 18**

"Are we going to church today, Daddy?" Alex asked, right after the blessing at breakfast.

"There aren't any churches around here," Kayla tried to answer.

"You're right, Kayla," Dad said, "but we're going anyway. We're going to one of God's most beautiful churches. We're going to take a picnic lunch and have church at Zion [zye-on] National Park."

"Where is that?" Alex asked.

"Oh, not too far away," Dad answered.

"Does it have big cliffs, like the place you and Zack went to the other day?" Kayla wanted to know.

"Even bigger," Dad promised. Then he saw the look on Mom's face. "But we're going to see them from the bottom of the canyon, not from the top."

"Are you sure the van will get us there?" Mom asked.

"Sure it will," he answered. "I hope."

Soon after starting we stopped at a crossroad. "OK, everyone, we have to decide here," Dad said. "There are two ways into Zion Canyon. The south road is pretty smooth and level and straight. But the east road winds down a curvy mountain trail and goes through a tunnel one mile long. Which one should we take?"

"Through the tunnel, through the tunnel," Alex, Kayla, and I shouted together.

"But it would take longer to get there," Dad warned.

"Tunnel! Tunnel!" we shouted again.

"But I might get carsick," he teased.

"Tunnel! Tunnel!"

"OK, OK," he laughed as he turned toward

the east road. Soon we were dropping down the twisting mountain road. It turned back and forth, back and forth, down toward the canyon. Many of the rocks here had strange shapes and bright colors too.

"Hey, Mom, look at that one. It looks like a red Christmas tree." I pointed out her window as I spoke.

"That's very nice, Zack," she said. She sounded funny. I looked at her more closely.

"Mom! You don't even have your eyes open."

"That's OK. Just tell me when we're at the bottom."

Soon we saw the dark mouth of the tunnel ahead. Dad turned on the headlights, and then we were swallowed up by the darkness. It did seem a little spooky to think that the mountain was on top of us. Especially when we couldn't see any light from either end of the tunnel.

But Mom seemed to like it. She even opened her eyes. "There aren't any bats in tunnels, are there?"

When we popped out into the sunshine of the canyon floor, everyone had their eyes wide open. The canyon was about as wide as a football field, and the walls went almost straight up on both sides. And I mean, they went a long way straight up.

DETECTIVE ZACK

A river flowed right through the middle, and beautiful green trees and grass grew on both sides. "Look," Kayla said, pointing out the window, "a deer. And there's another one." There they were, not afraid of the cars or people going by.

We explored for a while before lunch. "How far does this canyon go?" I asked Dad.

"Several miles. And farther on, it gets so narrow that you can reach across it and touch both sides. And in some places, the walls are almost 3,000 feet high."

After lunch, we sat together under a tree, next to the river, to have church. "We aren't having a sermon today. Let's just talk instead. Does anyone have an idea or a question we can discuss?"

I raised my hand. "Why do some scientists and teachers think the world is millions of years old? Are they just trying to trick us?"

Dad shook his head. "No, they're not trying to trick anyone. Many people, not just scientists and teachers, believe that the world is millions of years old. Some of them don't believe that there is a God, and some don't believe that the stories of Creation and the Flood in the Bible are true.

"Scientists have ways to measure how old rocks and things are. One way is called radiometric [ray-dee-o-met-rick] dating. It's hard to explain how they do it, but it tells them that many of the rocks and rock layers around here are millions of years old."

I was confused. "But how can they be right if the Bible is right?"

"There are two ways they could be right. How old was Adam when he was created, Kayla?" Dad asked.

Kayla said quickly, "One day old, of course."

"So he was a baby?" Mom asked.

"No, he was a grown-up. But he was only one day old. Right?"

Dad laughed. "It is kind of confusing. When God created Adam, He made him already grown up. It was just like Adam was already twenty or thirty years old. Maybe God did the same thing for the planet Earth."

"What do you mean?" Kayla asked.

"Maybe He created the world already old," I answered. "Could God do that, Dad?"

"I guess He could do anything He wanted. Maybe He created it like a planet millions of years old would be."

I got out my notebook to write. "What's the second way they could be right about the millions of years?"

"For that we need a Bible. Mom, did you bring

yours? I see that you did. Good. Let's let Alex read the first two verses of Genesis, the first two verses of the whole Bible."

Alex found it and read slowly. " 'In the beginning God created the heaven and the earth. And the earth was without form, and void; and darkness was upon the face of the deep. And the Spirit of God moved upon the face of the waters.' "

"Thank you, Alex. You read very well. Now, what do we know from those verses? Remember, God had not yet started the first day of creation. But what was already here?"

I thought about it. "Well, something was here. It was 'without form, and void,' whatever that means."

"That means that it was not shaped or finished, and nothing was on it. What else do the verses say?"

"The Spirit of God was here," Kayla added.

"Right. And what was He doing?"

Suddenly, the answer hit me like a cold shower. "Water! He was moving over the water—and God hadn't even started creating stuff yet."

"That's right, Zack," Dad said. "Before the week of Creation, the world was unfinished, but it was covered with water. Maybe it happened like this. Maybe when God began creating the universe,

He started with other parts of it and wasn't ready to work on the earth right away. So He rolled an extra blob of stuff over to one corner of space to wait—like you might roll a blob of Play-Doh to one side of the table until you were ready to work on it."

That made sense to me. "You're saying He waited to do the creating that Genesis talks about until the time was right."

"Exactly. So maybe the reason the rocks seem so old to scientists is that they really are millions of years old. Maybe they are part of the extra stuff God made the world out of."

Later, on the way back, we started having trouble. Yes, it was the van again. When we got to Cedar Breaks, it just wouldn't go any farther.

"Well, we'll wait here for it to cool down," Dad told Mom. "If it wasn't already dark, you could see down into the basin."

"That's OK. I don't mind," she said. "I wonder how long we'll have to wait. It's getting late."

We waited, but this time cooling off didn't help. The van moved out along the edge of the road, but it wouldn't go up the mountain. "I'll try and push while you drive," Dad told Mom as he got out.

"Do you think that's a good idea?" she asked, sliding into the driver's seat.

"It's the only idea I have left," he answered. He pushed on the back while Mom pushed on the gas pedal, but we still didn't go up the hill.

"I still have one idea," Mom said as he got back into the van. "Let's pray." And she did. "Father in heaven, please help us get back safely. Help us get our van over the mountain. Thank You, in Jesus' name. Amen."

We sat and waited. "If we could just make it over this last steep rise, we could coast down to Brian Head," Dad said.

I'm putting my notebook away for tonight. It looks like we are in deep trouble. Maybe it would help if I got out and pushed too. Or maybe we'll spend the night here on the side of the road.

Interesting Things I've Seen

A mile-long tunnel
Mule deer by the river
High, straight canyon walls

Important Words

Radiometric dating: A way scientists measure how old rocks and things are.
"Without form, and void": Not shaped or finished, and empty.

Noah's Flood Clues

An old earth: Scientists could be correct when they say that the world seems to be millions of years old. God might have created the world old, or He might have created it out of stuff He had made earlier, when He was working on other parts of the universe.

CHAPTER ELEVEN

Angels and Hoodoos

Field trip
Bryce Canyon National Park, Utah
July 19

I could have finished my cereal and toast. As usual, Dad rushed us out the door because we were going to be late; then we had to wait for him. So we sat in the van, waiting. And after last night, I'm not sure any of us wanted to get back into the van for another trip.

But Dad said he thought it'd be fine now. Of

course, that's what he said yesterday. And you know where that got us—stuck by the side of the road at Cedar Breaks in the middle of the night.

But what happened was pretty amazing.

In the few minutes after Mom had prayed for help, Dad and I tried pushing again. But that still didn't get us moving. Next we were going to open the hood and try to do something to the engine.

"Hey," Kayla called out from the back seat, "here comes a car."

From behind us, two headlights shone through the darkness. They came from an old, beat-up station wagon. It pulled over behind us on the side of the road, and two men got out. As they stepped into the beam of their headlights, I could see that they looked pretty beat-up too. They had old, dirty clothes and scruffy, dirty faces. I noticed that Mom leaned over and locked the van door.

"You folks got some kind of trouble?" The scruffy face produced a kind voice.

"Yes. Our van doesn't have enough power to get over this next rise. We're staying over in Brian Head, so if we could get over this last hump, we could coast in." Dad spoke in a friendly way as he explained. "Any chance you have a chain or rope that could pull us?"

The man looked over at his partner, who shook

his head. "No, I guess we don't. But we could push you if our bumpers match up."

"I don't think so. The bumpers on this minivan are probably higher than those on your station wagon."

"Let's try it and see," the man said and got into his station wagon. He pulled right up close behind us, until the bumpers were nearly touching.

"How about that! They are about the same height," Dad said. "Are you sure you want do this? If we move apart just a little and crash back together, it might damage your car."

"It'll be fine. Let's give it a try," the man said.

"OK," Dad replied. He got into the van, released the brakes, and put the shifter in neutral.

"Are you sure this is a good idea?" Mom asked.

"Even if it damages the bumper some, it won't cost that much. Not any more than it will cost to call a tow truck to come all the way out here. And this way we might get home tonight." As he spoke, I felt the station wagon bump the back, and then we were moving slowly up the hill.

We picked up speed as they pushed us faster. Then a little dip in the road made us move ahead of the station wagon. Dad slipped the car into gear and smashed the gas pedal to the floor. Nothing. The station wagon moved up from behind again.

"Hold on for a bump," Dad said. I grabbed Alex because he was looking back at the two men. The station wagon hit our bumper with a "thud," and then they were pushing us again. This time they stayed close to our van until we zipped over the top of the mountain.

"Here we go," Dad exclaimed. We pulled ahead of the station wagon and rolled down the slope.

"We're going to make it!" Mom said. I glanced back at the station wagon that was following at a distance. Alex was still staring at them. "I wish we could stop and thank them," Mom said.

"It wouldn't be smart to stop now. Besides, I don't remember any place to pull over until we get back to the town. When we get there, we'll stop to say thanks."

"They're gone," Alex said.

"What?"

"They're not there now. Their lights just went out." Alex was still looking back to where they had been.

"But they have to be. There was no place to turn, was there? And no houses where they could have stopped." I didn't understand.

Alex thought he did. "They must have been angels God sent to help us."

For a minute, no one said a word. My mouth

was hanging open like a flytrap. Then Mom said quietly, "Well, we did ask God for help."

When we were unloading the car, I saw Dad looking closely at the bumper. Then he looked up at me. "There's not a scratch or a dent," he said.

"Do you really think they were angels, Dad?"

"Well, it's kind of like the Flood story, Zack. You have to believe something. You can look at the evidence and decide that we were just lucky. They just happened to come along, and their car bumper just happened to match ours. We just got lucky when they bumped us and we didn't get a scratch. And they turned down some road we didn't see, or they turned around in the road and went back the way they came from.

"Or you can look at the same evidence and decide that whoever or whatever they were, God sent them along to help us."

Anyway, back to this morning. Dad finally made it to the van, and we followed the others in his class to Bryce Canyon. It's something like Cedar Breaks, only bigger and more colorful. And the rocks are in stranger shapes. One of Dad's teachers explained the view.

"Bryce Canyon is painted with more than sixty shades of red, pink, copper, and cream. And these strips of color seem to change as the sun moves across the sky. Some of the valleys between these colorful ridges are more than 1,000 feet deep."

He pointed at the rock shapes. "Some people see the forms of steeples, castles, or even animals in some of those strange shapes. But the really weird ones are called 'hoodoos.'"

"I think they look like castles," Mom said, with a dreamy look in her eyes. "Beautiful red-and-pink castles." I knew she would like the cliffs. But she did stay far back from the edge. To me, the formations all looked like hoodoos.

"What I want you to notice," the teacher went on, "is that cream-colored stripe near the top of the canyon wall. That layer of rock is found across four states. In some places it is pushed up in mountains. In other places it has been worn away by wind and rain. But that one layer of rock spreads out over more than 150,000 square miles."

"So what does that mean?" someone asked.

"The only place a layer like that could form today is at the bottom of the ocean. Only under water would there be similar conditions over that large an area. What I'm saying is that the best way to explain how such a large layer of rock was formed is—"

You guessed it. Noah's flood.

When we were on the way to our apartment,

Dad asked a question. "Zack, do you remember that floating stump we saw at the first campsite?"

I didn't remember. "Just a minute." I looked back in my notebook to the first few pages. And there it was, "one floating stump." I said, "I remember. We threw rocks at it. And we wondered if stumps always float straight up."

"Right. Do you remember what petrified wood is? That's wood that has turned to stone. Well, scientists were wondering about some petrified stumps they found in Yellowstone National Park. They were curious because so many were standing upright. Usually petrified trees are found fallen down, with their roots up in the air or broken off."

"And these stumps were all standing up like they were growing?" I asked.

"Yes," Dad said. "And scientists know they didn't turn to stone while they were still growing. So why are so many standing up straight?"

I knew this answer. "Because they were floating in water, like maybe in Noah's flood."

"That sounds like a good answer to me," Dad agreed.

That's why a good detective writes everything down. You never know when something strange will turn out to be an important clue.

Interesting Things I've Seen

"Hoodoos," or red-and-pink castles
Maybe two angels

Important Words

Petrified wood: Wood that has turned to stone, like a fossil.

Noah's Flood Clues

Big rock layers: Some layers of rock cover gigantic areas. Such large layers of rock could best be formed underwater. The best way to explain how that much land was underwater at the same time is Noah's flood.

Petrified stumps: Petrified stumps that are standing straight up could have been floating in the Flood until they settled into the mud.

CHAPTER TWELVE

Grand Canyon Clues

**Field trip
Grand Canyon National Park, Arizona
July 21**

"Dad, what did you do to fix the van?" I asked as I pulled out my notebook. We were almost to the Grand Canyon and were zipping right along. In fact, the van hadn't caused any problems for two days.

"Oh, I just opened the hood and adjusted a few things with a hammer," he said with a wink. "It

113

wouldn't dare give us any trouble now." It didn't, and we were soon parking at the Grand Canyon.

I'll tell you this—the Grand Canyon is big. I thought the other canyons we saw were amazing, but this one makes them look like cracks in a sidewalk. One of Dad's teachers explained how big.

"From this side of the Grand Canyon, the North Rim, you can see all the way to the South Rim because it is only about ten miles away. In some places, the canyon is eighteen miles wide."

"Oooooh," everyone said.

"The Grand Canyon is 277 miles long. In some places, it is one mile deep. That green ribbon you can barely see at the bottom is the Colorado River. The stripes of color on the canyon walls show the different layers of rock under our feet. The layers were laid down, one on top of the other, like frosting on a chocolate cake. And it was done either over millions of years or by Noah's flood."

When he was finished, I just stood there, staring down at the river. One thing was for sure. It either took a lot of water or a long time to dig a hole that big.

"Hey, Zack," Dad called, "come over here. I want to show you something."

I ran to where he was standing, close to the

edge. "You see that thick brown stripe of rock on the canyon wall?"

I looked. "OK. What about it?"

"See the white stripe on top of it? See how the white stripe fits on top of the brown one smooth and flat, like a white cover on a book with brown pages?"

I used his binoculars to follow the two stripes as far as I could along the canyon wall. "Yes. So?"

"There are fifteen million years between them!"

"What?" I was lost. I didn't know what he was talking about.

"According to the ages scientists figure those layers of rock to be, after the brown layer was formed, fifteen million years went by before the white rock was laid on top of it."

"So?"

"Look how flat they are!"

I still didn't understand.

"Let me explain it this way," he said. "If I were going to make you a basketball court at home, I'd measure out a place, fix boards around it, and have it filled with wet cement. Then I'd smooth the cement until it was nice and flat and level."

"That sounds like a good idea. Let's do it when we get home," I said. He just shook his head and went on talking.

"Then we'd have to try to keep everything and everyone off it until it dried and got hard, right? Any person or dog or cat that walked across it would leave marks. Even leaves or sticks would leave dips and bumps in the cement."

"How long would it take to dry and turn hard?" I asked.

"Probably one or two days. But what if it took one or two weeks? Do you think we could keep everything off it?"

"Maybe," I said.

"But what if it rained? That might wash some of it away."

"But it might not rain for two weeks," I reminded him.

"OK. But what about one or two years? Could we keep it smooth for that long?"

"No way. It would have all kinds of tracks and humps and holes in it by then." I was sure about that.

So was Dad. "You're right. But think about those rock layers over there again. When the brown layer was laid down, it was soft for a while. And even after it was hard, rain and wind and sand would be wearing it down to make it rough and uneven."

"OK. And how long do they say it was lying

there before the white level was added on top?"

"Fifteen million years. Somehow it lay there for fifteen million years in the sun and the rain —and it was still nice and smooth and level when the white layer was formed on top."

"That doesn't make sense," I said. "It should have been worn down in lots of places by then."

"It makes a lot more sense to think that those two layers were laid down one right after the other when a big flood stirred up a lot of mud."

Later, on the drive back, Dad told me more about the rock layers. "Scientists try to figure how long ago an animal lived by where in the rock layers they find fossils of it. Remember that fossils are formed when an animal dies and is covered by sand or mud. Later, when that sand or mud turns into rock, the skeleton or shell turns to stone also. Or a fossil can be formed like the dinosaur footprints we saw in Texas."

"Like when a cat steps in wet cement and the footprint is there after it gets hard." I knew how that was. Bobby's driveway has cat footprints in it.

"Right. So when a scientist sees an animal fossil in a rock layer, he says, 'That rock layer was formed twenty million years ago, so that animal lived twenty million years ago too.'"

"That makes sense," I said.

"Maybe so," said Dad, "but listen to this. The most recent fossils scientists had found of what they called the tuatara [too-uh-ta-ruh], a reptile that looks like a lizard, were in rock layers they figured were 135 million years old. So they thought that the tuatara had died out 135 million years ago—until some living ones were found on a New Zealand island."

"Real, live ones?"

"Yes. And they looked almost the same as the fossil tuataras. So using fossils to decide how long ago an animal lived doesn't always work."

"If some animals living today look almost the same as their fossils, then either animals don't change much as time goes by or else not much time has gone by," I said.

"It's not hard for me to believe that they look the same today as they did before Noah's flood," Dad agreed. "In fact, I think it makes a lot of sense."

I was writing in my notebook when Alex spoke up. "Dad, I miss our dog, Murphy. Do you think he's OK?"

"You can find out yourself soon. We're leaving for home tomorrow."

"Are we driving straight home without stopping?" Kayla asked.

"No, we still have places to stop and things to see," Dad answered. "But we need to start on the road home. How about it, detective? Is the case nearly solved? Are we ready to go?"

I looked at my nearly full notebook. "Let's go home. I've got a lot to show someone about science and the Bible."

Interesting Things I've Seen

A very, very big canyon
Layers of rock that look like frosting on a cake
A green-ribbon river

Important Words

Fossil: What's left when a skeleton or body or the mud around a footprint turns to rock.

Tuatara: A kind of reptile that looks the same as its "135-million-year-old" fossil relatives.

Noah's Flood Clues

Living fossils: Either the tuatara reptile hasn't changed much in 135 million years or a lot less time has gone by.

Smooth rock layers: How could they be so smooth and flat where they touch if they weren't both laid down at the same time?

CHAPTER THIRTEEN

The Case Is Closed

**On the freeway
Somewhere in West Virginia
July 25**

I'm not sure what woke me up, the screeching tires or the suitcase that fell on my head.

"What happened?" I pushed the suitcase off and tried to get up. We were stopped on the side of the road. Dad's door slammed as I sat up. He walked by my window to the back of the van.

Mom turned and smiled at me. "It's OK, Zack.

DETECTIVE ZACK

A deer ran out in front of us, but we swerved and missed him—I think. Kayla, are you OK?"

I pulled a sleeping bag away from the seat where Kayla was sleeping. "Kayla? Are you still there?"

Her sleepy voice came up from under her blanket. "Mom, tell Zack to stop pushing things on me. I'm trying to sleep."

I looked at Mom. She laughed. "I guess she's all right. Where's Alex? Is he OK?"

I looked over to where Alex was. He hadn't even stopped snoring. "He's still asleep, Mom." It takes more than almost crashing to wake him up. I guess little brothers are just like that.

Dad climbed back in. "We must have missed the deer. I don't see any sign of it or any marks on the van. It sure was close, though. I'm glad home is only two hours away."

For some reason, I didn't feel sleepy anymore. But Mom was yawning.

"Mom, if you're sleepy, I'll sit up there, and you can rest back here on the seat."

"Thanks, Zack. I am sleepy." She crawled back and I climbed over until we were settled.

The clock on the car radio said it was midnight. "Hey, buddy, be sure your seat belt is on," Dad said as I settled in with my notebook and pillow.

"So Detective Zack," he asked, "are you ready to close the case? Do you think the Bible story of the Flood is true?"

I looked at my notebook. "When you see the way the earth is put together, Noah's flood makes the most sense. With the rock layers and the deep canyons, the Bible has the best answer. You can look around and see clues everywhere that a big flood really happened."

"So what do you think Bobby will say? Will he believe the Flood story is true too?"

I waved my notebook around. "He has to! When I show him all these clues, he'll know I was right."

"Zack, what is the biggest difference between you and Bobby?" Dad stared ahead as he asked.

"Well, he is one inch taller than I. And we go to different schools and . . . I guess we believe different things."

"The biggest difference is that you've been raised to believe in God, and Bobby hasn't. He has always been taught that science and scientists have the answers to questions about where we came from and why we are here on earth."

"But his 'millions of years' idea doesn't fit all the clues! There are a lot of questions it can't answer. It has big problems." I was sure Bobby could see that.

"But what if a person doesn't believe in God?" Dad asked quietly.

I had to think about that for a while. The Flood was only possible if God made it happen. "I guess if you don't believe in God, evolution's millions of years is probably the best idea you'll find."

"I'm afraid you're right," Dad agreed. "But do you think Bobby will understand why you believe in Noah's flood?"

"I think so. At least he'll know that the Flood could have happened." I sat for a minute, watching the stars through the window. "Dad, why didn't God just give us proof that the Flood happened so everyone would know that the Bible is true? Wouldn't it be easier?"

"God built His whole universe around two things, Zack—love and freedom. He wants everyone to be free to choose what to believe. He loves them enough to let them choose," Dad explained. "He doesn't force anyone to believe. He just gives enough clues that anyone can have faith and believe if they choose to."

I was confused. "So I shouldn't try to show Bobby that the Flood is true?"

"Tell him about the clues you found. But don't worry about making him believe it. The most important thing to show Bobby is that God is real and that God loves him," Dad said.

"How can I do that?"

"By just being his friend and treating him with kindness," Dad answered. "And when you have a chance, tell him about God."

"And invite him to church once in a while?"

Dad nodded. "Sure. Now, why don't you get some sleep."

"OK. I just want to write a few more things in my notebook." I shined my flashlight on the last pages of my notebook so I could see to write.

It made sense that a flood that covered the whole world would leave some clues. You can't make a mess that big without leaving a mark! So I'm not surprised to learn that scientists have found flood clues.

I guess Dad's right. I believe all these clues point to Noah's flood because I believe in God. But when you add up all the clues, it's easy to believe what the Bible says. I'm glad I know the truth, and I'm glad I know that God loves me. It's nice to know that He doesn't force anyone to believe. He lets me make up my own mind.

I guess God is just like that.

Wait a minute. My flashlight batteries are going dead again! Should I ask Dad for more? No, I'll wait and finish this tomorrow.

Interesting Things I've Seen

I've seen that compared to the Bible, evolution's millions-of-years idea is pretty weak.

I've seen that the most important thing is finding out that God is real and that He loves us.

Important Words

Love: What God has for everyone.

Freedom: You get to choose for yourself what to believe.

Noah's Flood Clues

My conclusion: The clues don't prove that Noah's flood really happened, but seeing all the evidence makes me believe it did.

Dad, I need more batteries again. But there's no hurry—unless we're going on another trip soon!